INVINCIBLE WISDOM

Quotations from the
Scriptures, Saints, and Sages
of All Times and Places

Compiled by William Stoddart

INVINCIBLE WISDOM: Quotations from the Scriptures, Saints, and
Sages of All Times and Places
© 2008 by William Stoddart

For information, address:
Sophia Perennis,
P.O. Box 151011
San Rafael, CA 94915
sophiaperennis.com

Library of Congress Cataloging-in-Publication Data

Invincible Wisdom : Quotations from the Scriptures, Saints, and Sages
of all Times and Places / compiled by William Stoddart. – 1st ed.

p. cm.
Includes index.
ISBN 978-1-59731-088-8 (pbk. : alk. paper)

1. Religion–Quotations, maxims, etc.
2. Spiritual life–Quotations, maxims, etc.
I. Stoddart, William.
PN6084.R3I58 2008
200–dc22   2008022411

Other Books by the Same Author

Remembering in a World of Forgetting: Thoughts on Tradition and Postmodernism
(World Wisdom Books, Bloomington, Indiana, 2008)

Hinduism and its Spiritual Masters
(first edition, 1993; second edition, Fons Vitae, Louisville, Kentucky, 2007)

Outline of Buddhism
(Foundation for Traditional Studies, Oakton, Virginia, 1998)

Sufism: The Mystical Doctrines and Methods of Islam
(first edition, 1976; latest reprint: Paragon House, Saint Paul, Minnesota, 1985)

Contents

Preface

An anthology, by definition, cannot be complete, but this does not mean that it must be arbitrary. An anthology that contains some beautiful poems does not lack meaning or value merely because other beautiful poems have been excluded. On the contrary, to the degree that the anthology is shaped by a guiding idea, the selection, far from being arbitrary, becomes a qualitative entity, and takes on a distinct and meaningful character of its own.

This also applies to an anthology of quotations: the choice can never be completely arbitrary, for always "there is method in it". In the present case the "method" — the guiding idea — has been to gather together sayings, maxims, and aphorisms, which, in some respect or other, are of profound and permanent spiritual value. Moreover, the net has been cast wide, with the result that the selected items are extremely variegated; for, in the present age, protective dividing walls have crumbled; the whole world has become our parish, and our gaze must now be universal.

I have occasionally supplied the original language (Sanskrit, Greek, Latin, Italian, Spanish, French, German, or Arabic, as the case may be) of a given quotation. This is chiefly to lend additional "strength" to the quotation in question, and also to provide some linguistic enjoyment for those who are interested.

On one or two occasions, a quotation appears in two places. I have let this stand, because it seemed appropriate, in these few cases, that a given quotation should be presented in two different contexts or settings.

The quotations here presented were collected during the course of a lifetime. Each quotation was hand-picked for a particular reason, and anything deemed superfluous was excluded. Wise and useful quotations are of course endless, but a selection is what it is and, far from being arbitrary, this anthology, taken as a whole, amounts to a succinct, but powerful, affirmation of "the True, the Good, and the Beautiful". This is its purpose — and may it bear fruit.

William Stoddart

Introduction

The age we live in is certainly not one that engenders tranquillity or reassurance. Indisputably it is an age of dissatisfaction, agitation, and revolt. It is an age which, paradoxically, combines a shallow optimism with a deep *Angst*.

It is obvious to many that all is not right. But what is it that has gone wrong? What is really at the bottom of this rushing, ever-changing, never-stationary modern age?

One of the most obvious features of the present is our oblivion of the past — even of the recent past. We no longer look to the accumulated experience of yesteryear, or to a pre-existing corpus of wisdom, for guidance. On the contrary, we are encouraged not to turn to the past, but to start each new day with a *tabula rasa*, a clean sheet. The trouble with this is that "nature abhors a vacuum" and, inevitably, something will come to fill it. It might be inane, but slyly seductive advertising; it might be fleeting, but deliberately misleading "sound-bites"; it might be any one of the many corrupting superficialities which today invade our personal space and influence our life. Whatever it may be, the order of the day is always agitation and change. This state of affairs is said to be "freedom of choice", or "freedom from superstition and dogma"; but some already suspect that it is a very shallow freedom, one that visibly fails to give us tranquillity, stability, or hope. The age we live in is one which, in an inhuman and unprecedented manner, rejects all tradition; it is an age of which the principal characteristic is forgetfulness. The logical antidote to forgetfulness is obviously "remembering". But remembering what?

To a generation deprived of its cultural heritage and of anything approaching a normal formation, the present collection of quotations will be an eye-opener. It is both an education and an invitation: it is an *education*, because it brings the modern reader, perhaps for the first time, into close contact with some of humanity's truly great — the bearers and teachers of the wisdom of the ages; and it is an *invitation* to remember — to remember a rich past, which is now all but forgotten, but which constitutes one of the necessary keys for distancing ourselves from the downward rush towards ever-increasing superficiality, quantification, and despair.

The present collection consists principally of sayings of the Greeks, the Romans, the Medievals, the Scriptures, and the wise men of East and West. Dear reader, have courage! Be not afraid! The sayings here anthologized are not out-moded, out-dated, or difficult to understand. Most of them are of a blinding clarity; they are universal and perennial; they combine a lofty vision with a homely wisdom that all can grasp.

I need not go on: the message is contained in the sayings themselves: they are a solace, a medicine, and a cure.

(1) Biblical Quotations

To every thing there is a season, and a time to every purpose under the heaven: a time to be born, and a time to die; a time to plant and a time to pluck up that which is planted; a time to kill and a time to heal; a time to break down and a time to build up; a time to weep and a time to laugh; a time to mourn and a time to dance; a time to cast away stones and a time to gather stones together; a time to embrace and a time to refrain from embracing; a time to get and a time to lose; a time to keep and a time to cast away; a time to rend and a time to sew; a time to keep silence and a time to speak; a time to love and a time to hate; a time of war and a time of peace.

Ecclesiastes, **3, 1-8**

The fool hath said in his heart: there is no God.

Psalms of David, **14, 1**

The man that wandereth from the way of true doctrine shall remain in the congregation of the dead.

Proverbs, **21, 16**

The kingdom of God cometh not with observation.

Luke, **17, 20**

And if the blind lead the blind, both shall fall into the ditch.

Matthew, **15, 14**

This is an evil generation: they seek a sign; and there shall no sign be given it.

Luke, **11, 29**

For there shall arise false Christs, and false prophets, and shall show great signs and wonders; insomuch that, if it were possible, they shall deceive the very elect.

Matthew, **24, 24**

Many will say to me in that day: Lord, Lord, have we not prophesied in thy Name? and in thy Name cast out devils? and in thy Name done many wonderful works? And then will I profess unto them: I never knew you; depart from me, ye that work iniquity.

Matthew, **7, 22-23**

But he that shall endure unto the end, the same shall be saved.

Matthew, **24, 13**

It must needs be that scandals come, but woe to that man through whom the scandal cometh.

Matthew, **18, 7**

Behold, I have told you beforehand.

Matthew, **24, 25**

There shall come in the last days scoffers, walking after their own lusts. And saying: "Where is the promise of his coming? For since the fathers fell asleep, all things continue as they were from the beginning of creation." For this they willingly are ignorant. . . .

2 Peter, **3, 3-5**

Think not that I am come to send peace on earth; I came not to send peace, but a sword.

Matthew, **10, 34**
(See also *Luke,* 22, 36-38)

Regnum Dei intra vos est.

The kingdom of God is within you.

Luke, **17, 21**

Sine intermissione orate.

Pray without ceasing.

1 Thessalonians, **5, 17**

And Peter opened his mouth and said: "Truly I perceive that God shows no partiality, but in every nation any one who fears Him and does what is right is acceptable to Him."

Acts, **10, 34-35**

For ye, brethren, became followers of the churches of God which in Judea are in Christ Jesus: for ye also have suffered like things of your own countrymen, even as they have of the Jews: who both killed the Lord Jesus, and their own prophets, and have persecuted us; and they please not God, and are contrary to all men.

1 Thessalonians, **2, 14-15**

For the children of this world are in their generation wiser than the children of light.

Luke, **16, 8**

By their fruits ye shall know them.

Matthew, 7, 20

My people are destroyed for lack of knowledge. Because thou hast rejected knowledge, I will also reject thee.

Hosea, 4, 6

Woe unto them that call evil good, and good evil; that put darkness for light, and light for darkness.

Isaiah, 5, 20

We wrestle not against flesh and blood, but against principalities, against powers, against the rulers of the darkness of this world, against spiritual wickedness in high places.

Ephesians, 6, 12-15

Kaì gnósesthe tèn 'alétheian kaì he 'alétheia 'eleutherósei hemãs.
Cognoscetis veritatem et veritas liberabit vos.

Ye shall know the truth and the truth shall make you free.

John, 8, 32

Nisi Dominus aedificaverit domum, frustra laboraverunt qui aedificant eam.

Unless the Lord build the house, they labor in vain that build it.

Psalms, 127, 1

The deceitfulness of riches choketh the word.

Matthew, 13, 22

The poor ye shall always have with you.
John, **12, 8**

Martha, Martha, thou art careful and troubled about many things, but one thing is needful: and Mary hath chosen that good part, which shall not be taken away from her.
Luke, **10, 41-42**

Be zealous for the better gifts. I show you a more excellent way.
1 Corinthians, **12, 31**

Man shall not live by bread alone, but by every word that proceedeth out of the mouth of God.
Matthew, **4, 4**

What is a man profited, if he shall gain the whole world, and lose his own soul?
Matthew, **16, 26**

Seek ye first the kingdom of God and his righteousness, and all these things shall be added unto you.
Matthew, **6, 33**

Where your treasure is, there will your heart be also.
Matthew, **6, 21**

Woe unto you, when all men shall speak well of you! For so did their fathers to the false prophets.

Luke, **6, 26**

What all men speak well of, look critically into.

Confucius

If thou see a man of understanding, go to him early in the morning, and let thy feet wear out his doorstep.

Ecclesiasticus, **6, 36**

(2) Quotations from the Koran

To God belong the East and the West; wheresoever ye may turn, there is the Face of God.

Sûrat al-Baqara,
Chapter "The Cow", 2, 115

God is the Light of the Heavens and the earth.

Sûrat an-Nûr,
Chapter "Light", 24, 35

We created the Heavens and the earth with naught but Truth, yet most men know not.

Sûrat ad-Dukhân,
Chapter "Smoke", 44, 38-39

Everything on earth shall pass away; there abideth but the Face of thy Lord, resplendent with Majesty and Bounty.

Sûrat ar-Rahmân,
Chapter "The All-Merciful", 55, 26-27

You will find that the best friends of believers [i.e. Muslims] are those who say: "We are Christians." This is because there are priests and monks amongst them, and because they are not proud.

Sûrat al-Mâ'ida,
Chapter "The Table", 5, 82

Only they are true believers whose hearts tremble when God is mentioned; who, when the revelations of God are recited to them, increase their faith, and trust in their Lord; who engage in prayer, and give freely of that which We have bestowed on them. These are the true believers; for them are grades of honor with their Lord, and pardon, and a bountiful provision.

Sûrat al-Anfâl,
Chapter "The Spoils", 8, 2-4

Yurîdûna li-yutfi'u nûra 'Llâhi bi-afwâi-him, wa 'Llâhu mutimmu nûri-hi wa lau kariha 'l-kâfirûn.

They seek to extinguish God's light by blowing it out, but God will perfect His light, even though this may not please unbelievers.

Sûrat as-Saff,
Chapter "The Ranks", 61, 8

In every nation we have raised a Messenger, proclaiming: Serve God and shun false gods.

Sûrat al-Nahl,
Chapter "The Bee", 16, 36

Truth has come, and falsehood has vanished. Verily falsehood is ever bound to vanish.

Sûrat Banî Isrâ'îl,
Chapter "The Children of Israel", 17, 81

It is not their eyes that are blind, but their hearts.

Sûrat al-Hajj,
Chapter "The Pilgrimage", 22, 46

O Mankind! We created you from a single (pair) of a male and a female, and made you into nations and tribes that ye may know each other (not that ye may despise each other).

Sûrat al-Hujurât,
Chapter "The Private Apartments",
49, 13

Al-hamdu li 'Llâhi 'lladhi hadâ-nâ li-hadhâ, wa mâ kunnâ li-nahtadiya, lau lâ hadâ-nâ 'Llâh.

Praise be to God who has guided us to this; we could not have been rightly guided, if God had not guided us.

Sûrat al-A'râf,
Chapter "Discernment", 7, 43

Fa 'stamsi-ka bi 'lladhi ûhiya ilai-ka. Inna-ka 'alâ sirâtim mustaqîm.

Hold fast to that which is inspired in thee. Verily thou art on the right path.

Sûrat az-Zuhruf,
Chapter "Gold", 43, 43

There is no compulsion in religion.

Sûrat al-Baqara,
Chapter "The Cow", 2, 256

With God, there is no coercion.

Saint Irenaeus of Lyons (2nd century)

(3) Hermes Trismegistos

The Greek god Hermes or Mercury, "keeper and revealer of Supreme Knowledge", is identified with the Egyptian god Thoth. Hermes was the figure upon whom the ancient Egyptian priests modeled themselves. It is from Hermes that the intellectual and spiritual current known as Hermetism takes its name. Hermes Trismegistos (the "Thrice-Great Hermes") is said to have been the originator of a series of works in Greek known as the *Corpus Hermeticum*, which appeared in Alexandria at the end of the Hellenic period. Hermetism is a sapiential or *jñânic* doctrine of salvation. The *Corpus Hermeticum* contains seventeen short tracts, one of which, *Poimandres*, teaches that the initiator is the *Nous* or Supreme Intellect. The *Corpus Hermeticum* enjoyed great popularity during the Middle Ages, and was rediscovered by the Neoplatonists of the Renaissance. Another content of the *Corpus Hermeticum* is the "Emerald Tablet", which enshrines the following declaration:

(*Taken in part from* "Les Maîtres Spirituels" *by Jacques Brosse*)

FIRST: I speak not false things, but only what is certain and true.

SECOND: That which is below is like unto that which is above, and that which is above is like unto that which is below, to produce the miracle of the One Sole Thing.

THIRD: As all things come from the one Word of one Being, so all things come from this by adaptation.

FOURTH: Its Father is the Sun, its Mother is the Moon, the Wind carries it in its belly, and its Nurse is the Earth.

FIFTH: It is the Father of every perfection in the world.

SIXTH: The Power is great if it be changed into earth.

SEVENTH:	Separate earth from fire, the subtle from the gross, gently and with great care.
EIGHTH:	Ascend with great intelligence from earth to heaven, descend again to earth, and unite the powers of the higher and lower things. Thus will you receive the glory of the universe, and darkness will flee from you.
NINTH:	This has more strength than strength itself, for it overcomes everything subtle and penetrates everything solid.
TENTH:	Thus was the world formed.
ELEVENTH:	Hence come the wonders here established.
TWELFTH:	Therefore I am named Hermes Trismegistos, having the three parts of the philosophy of the whole world.
THIRTEENTH:	That which I had to say concerning the Sun's operation is finished.

Sentences from the *Corpus Hermeticum*

As bodies are reflected in mirrors, so incorporeal things are reflected in bodies. The intelligible Cosmos is reflected in the sensible cosmos. Therefore, my King, worship the statues of the gods, seeing that these statues too have in them forms which come from the intelligible Cosmos.

You will be led to the knowledge of the inward things which are invisible to you, by the outward things which you see before you. And so, we can represent to ourselves in thought the Author of all that is, by contemplating the visible things which were made by Him.

This world is a place for the learning of Truth. The visible forms which it presents to our senses are fleeting and perishable, but they are semblances or shadows of forms which, though not apprehensible by the senses, are real and everlasting.

You say: "God is invisible"? Say not so. Who is more manifest than God? For this very purpose has he made all things, that through all things you may see him. This is God's goodness, that he manifests himself through all things.

The deceptive and fleeting pleasures of the sense-world suggest to us that we should turn from them to the true and unceasing pleasures of the Noetic or Intellectual world. The frail, transitory, and perishable forms of the sense-world bid us turn from them to the stable and constant forms of the Intellectual world.

By the light of the Intellect the human soul is illumined, as the world is illumined by the sun — nay, in yet fuller measure.

The vice of the soul is ignorance.

If you learn to know yourself as life and light, you will return to life.

He who knows how to lose well wins; he who knows not how to win well, loses.

(4) Some Sayings of Confucius
(551-479 B.C.)

The wise man, in his attitude towards the world, has neither predilections not prejudices. He is on the side of what is right.

Knowledge without thinking is useless. Thinking without knowledge is dangerous.

Tzû Kung said: Our Master's culture and refinement all may hear: but our Master's discourse on the nature of man and the laws of Heaven is not given to all to hear.

The people may be made to follow a course, but not to understand the reason for it.

What all men speak well of, look critically into; what all men condemn, examine first before you decide.

What would you say of the person who is liked by all his fellow townsmen? That is not sufficient. What is better is that the good among his fellow townsmen like him, and the bad hate him.

There are few who understand virtue.

The firm of spirit, the resolute in character, the simple in manner, and the slow of speech are not far from virtue.

Is virtue indeed far off? I crave for virtue, and lo! virtue is at hand.

If one attacks one's own failings rather than those of others, that will remedy one's personal faults.

The men of old were reserved in speech out of shame, lest they should become short in deed.

The well-bred are dignified, but not pompous; the ill-bred are pompous, but not dignified.

In the arts of civilization, our ancestors are considered by some to have been uncultured, while their successors are considered to be cultured. But when I have need of these arts, I follow our ancestors.

He who is in harmony with Nature hits the mark without effort and apprehends the truth without hesitation.

What is the art of government?
The art of government simply consists in making things right, and putting things in their right places.

He who exercises government by means of his virtue may be compared to the north polar star which keeps its place and all the stars turn towards it.

In periods of disorder, rites are altered and music is licentious. Then sad sounds lack dignity, and joyful sounds lack calm. . . . When the spirit of opposition manifests itself, indecent music comes into being.

When you see the type of a nation's dance, you know its character.

By three methods we may learn wisdom: First, by reflection, which is noblest; second, by imitation, which is easiest; and third by experience, which is the bitterest.

The only one to argue with a fool is a bigger fool.

(5) Hymn by Shankara

Eight stanzas addressed to the
Divine Mother (*Bhavani*)

by Shankara
(the greatest of the Hindu sages, c. 788-820)

1

No father have I, no mother, no comrade,
No son, no daughter, no wife, and no grandchild,
No servant, no master, no wisdom, no calling:

> *In Thee is my only haven of refuge,*
> *In Thee, my help and my strength, O Bhavani!*

2

Immersed as I am in the limitless ocean
Of worldly existence, I tremble to suffer.
Alas! I am lustful and foolish and greedy,
And ever enchained by the fetters of evil:

> *In Thee is my only haven of refuge,*
> *In Thee, my help and my strength, O Bhavani!*

3

To giving of alms and to meditation,
To scriptures and hymns and mantras, a stranger,
I know not of worship, possess no dispassion:

> *In Thee is my only haven of refuge,*
> *In Thee, my help and my strength, O Bhavani!*

4

O Mother! Of pilgrimage and of merit,
Of mental control and of the soul's liberation,
Of rigorous vows and of devotion, I know not:

In Thee is my only haven of refuge,
In Thee, my help and my strength, O Bhavani!

5

Addicted to sinning and worthless companions,
A slave to ill thoughts and to doers of evil,
Degraded am I, unrighteous, abandoned,
Attached to ill objects, adept at ill-speaking:

In Thee is my only haven of refuge,
In Thee, my help and my strength, O Bhavani!

6

I know neither Brahma nor Vishnu not Shiva,
Nor Indra, nor Surya, nor Chandra, nor similar Being —
Not one of the numberless gods, O Redeemer!

In Thee is my only haven of refuge,
In Thee, my help and my strength, O Bhavani!

7

In strife or in sadness, abroad or in danger,
In water, in fire, in the wilds, in the mountains,
Surrounded by foes, my Savior, protect me!

> *In Thee is my only haven of refuge,*
> *In Thee, my help and my strength, O Bhavani!*

8

Defenseless am I — ill, aging, and helpless,
Enfeebled, exhausted, and dumbly despairing,
Afflicted with sorrow, and utterly ruined:

> *In Thee is my only haven of refuge,*
> *In Thee, my help and my strength, O Bhavani!*

Innumerable evils have encompassed me about: mine iniquities have taken hold upon me, so that I am not able to look up; they are more than the hairs of mine head; therefore my heart faileth me.

Be pleased, O Lord, to deliver me: O Lord, make haste to help me.
Psalms of David, 40, 12-13

---

(6) Some Sayings of the Prophet Mohammed

No hour passes by for the son of Adam in which he fails to remember God but that he regrets it on the Day of Resurrection.

The Friends of God are those who, when they are seen, cause
one to remember God.

Inna li-kulli shai'in siqâlatan wa siqâlatu 'l-qulûbi dhikru 'Llâh.

For every thing there is a polish and the polish for hearts is the
remembrance of God.

When the Prophet was asked which spiritual strivers would receive
the greatest reward, he replied: "Those who remember God
most." And when the prayer was mentioned, and the almsgiving
was mentioned, and the pilgrimage, the charitable donations,
and the fast were mentioned, he said of each: "The richest in the
remembrance of God is the richest in reward."

All who live in this world are asleep, and when they die they
awaken.

Li-kulli maliki khazâna, khazânatî fî 'l-ardi qalbu 'abdî 'l-mu'min.

Every king has a treasury; My treasury on earth is the heart of My
believing slave.
> (a *hadîth qudsî*, a "Divine Saying" from
> the mouth of Mohammed)

The superiority of the gnostic (*'âlim*) over the obedientialist
(*'âbid*) is as the superiority of the full moon over the other
heavenly bodies.

O Lord, make us to see things as they are.

A man asked Mohammed: "O Messenger of God, who has the greatest right to my companionship in good spirit?" Mohammed replied: "Thy mother." The man asked again: "Then who?" He answered: "Thy mother." Again the man asked: "Then who?" He answered: "Thy mother." Once more he asked: "Then who?" Mohammed said: "Thy father."

The seeking of knowledge is obligatory upon every Muslim man and woman.

(*See the quotation from Hosea on p. 5.*)

Whoso protecteth God in his heart, him will God protect in the world.

A man may dwell among the people of prayer, almsgiving, and pilgrimage until he is counted among those to whom Paradise is apportioned, but he will not be rewarded on the Day of Resurrection except to the degree of his intelligence.

Worship God as if thou sawest Him, for, if thou seest Him not, verily He seeth thee.

Following a battle against the opponents of the new religion, Mohammed said to his companions: "We are returning from the *lesser holy war* [against our outward enemies] to the *greater holy war* [against our inward enemies — the temptations that are ever present within our souls]."

Inna 'Llâha jamîlun, yuhibbu 'l-jamâl.
Verily God is beautiful and He loves beauty.

Ikhtilâfu 'l-'ulamâ'i rahma.

Diversity of opinion amongst scholars (or experts or authorities) is a blessing.

Some Traditional Arab Sayings

Ya mani 'smu-hu dawâ' wa dhikru-hu shifâ'.

O Thou whose Name is a medicine and whose remembrance is a cure.

The beauty of man is in his intelligence and the intelligence of woman is in her beauty.

A Saying which the Islamic Tradition
attributes to Jesus

Jesus, on whom be blessings and peace, was traveling with his companions, when they came upon the rotting carcass of an ass. The companions were offended by the decomposing body and voiced their disgust. But Jesus said unto them: "Did ye not perceive the ivory of its teeth?"

Fallen man sees, and is ensnared by, the corruptible; but the spiritual man, on the pattern of Jesus, goes straight to the incorruptible, and fixes on it. He discriminates between the permanent and the impermanent, and concentrates on the permanent.

(7) Islamic Quotations

My Lord, eyes are at rest, the stars are setting, hushed are the movements of the birds in their nests, of the monsters in the deep. And Thou art the Just, who knoweth no change, the Equity that swerveth not, the Everlasting that passeth not away. The doors of kings are locked and guarded by their henchmen. But Thy door is open to whoso calleth on Thee. My Lord, each lover is now alone with his beloved. And I am alone with Thee.

Hudhaifa al-'Adawîya (8th century)
(often attributed to Râbi'a al-'Adawîya)

When an anchorite goes into a tavern, the tavern becomes his cell, and when a haunter of taverns goes into a cell, that cell becomes his tavern.

Hujwîrî (died 1071)

He who knows God, loves Him, and he who knows the world, flees from it.

Hasan al-Basrî (died 728)

This place is the shrine of Divine lovers; those coming incomplete are completed here.

Jâmî (1414-1492)
(Couplet displayed at the mausoleum of Rûmî at Konya, Turkey)

I am neither Christian nor Jew nor Parsi nor Muslim. I am neither of the East nor of the West, neither of the land nor of the sea. . . . I have put aside duality and have seen that the two worlds are one. I seek the One, I know the One, I see the One, I invoke the One. He is the First, He is the Last, He is the Outward, He is the Inward.

Rûmî (1207-1273)

If one of my friends is in danger, I will save him, whether I be in this world or the next. For my horse is saddled, my lance is ready, my sword is drawn, and my bow is bent for the protection of my companions and friends, even if they be completely unaware of this!

'Abd al-Qâdir al-Jîlânî (1078-1166)

If thou wouldst become a pilgrim of love, the first condition is that thou become as humble as dust.

Ansari (1006-1089)

For Thy sake I haste over land and water, over plain and mountain, and from everything I meet, I turn my face, until the time when I reach that place where I am alone with Thee.

Niffârî (died 965)

Mâ ladhatu 'l-'aîshi illâ suhbatu 'l-fuqarâ.
Humu 's-sulâtînu wa 's-sâdâtu wa 'l-ûmarâ.

There is no happiness in life except in the company of *fuqarâ*. They are Sultans, Lords, and Emirs!

(*fuqarâ* = the poor in spirit)
Shu'aib Abu Madyan (died c. 1197)

On entering Fez, one can see on the right the green tiles under which repose the remains of the renowned Sufi As-Sanûsî, a sensitive, timid, and delicate man of God, who instructed his disciples not to crush any insects that might lie in their path, and amongst whose singular virtues is listed the fact that he gave back borrowed books to their owners long before it had occurred to them to ask for their return.

As-Sanûsî
extract from *Le Culte des Saints dans l'Islam maghrébin*
by Émile Dermenghem (Paris, Gallimard, 1954, pp. 82-83)

God did not distribute to His servants anything more to be esteemed than Intelligence.

'Alî (the Fourth Caliph of Islam)

Know that this world was not made for you to live in forever. You will have to exchange it for the hereafter. God did not create you without purpose, and has not left you without obligations and responsibilities.

'Alî (the Fourth Caliph of Islam)

Seekest thou Laila [Divine Reality], when she is manifest within thee? Thou deemest her to be other, but she is not other than thou.

Mohammed al-Harrâq (died 1845)

(8) The Ninety-Nine Names of God

The Ninety-Nine Names of God as taught in Islam:
"To God belong the most beautiful Names; invoke Him by them."
(Wa li 'Llâhi 'l-asmâ'u 'l-husnâ, fa 'd'û-hu bi-hâ.)
Koran, Chapter "The Heights", 7, 180

Allâh = God

(1) *ar-Rahmân* = the Clement

(2) *ar-Rahîm* = the Merciful

(3) *al-Malik* = the King

(4) *al-Quddûs* = the Holy

(5) *as-Salâm* = the Peace

(6) *al-Mu'min* = the Faithful

(7) *al-Muhaimin* = the Protector

(8) *al-'Azîz* = the Mighty

(9) *al-Jabbâr* = the Repairer

(10) *al-Mutakabbir* = the Great

(11) *al-Khâliq* = the Creator

(12) *al-Barî* = the Maker

(13) *al-Musawwir* = the Fashioner

(14) *al-Ghaffâr* = the Forgiver

(15) *al-Qahhâr* = the Dominant

(16) *al-Wahhâb* = the Bestower

(17) *ar-Razzâq* = the Provider

(18) *al-Fattâh* = the Opener

(19) *al-'Alîm* = the Knower

(20) *al-Qâbiz* = the Restrainer

(21) *al-Bâsit* = the Spreader

(22) *al-Khâfiz* = the Abaser

(23) *al-Râfi'* = the Exalter

(24) *al-Mu'izz* = the Honorer

(25) *al-Muzîl* = the Destroyer

(26) *as-Sâmi'* = the Hearer

(27) *al-Basîr* = the Seer

(28) *al-Hâkim* = the Ruler

(29) *al-'Âdl* = the Just

(30) *al-Latîf* = the Subtle

(31) *al-Khabir* = the Aware

(32) *al-Halîm* = the Sweet

(33) *al-'Azîm* = the Mighty

(34) *al-Ghafûr* = the Forgiving

(35) *ash-Shakûr* = the Grateful

(36) *al-'Alî* = the Exalted

(37) *al-Kabîr* = the Great

(38) *al-Hâfiz* = the Guardian

(39) *al-Muqît* = the Strengthener

(40) *al-Hasîb* = the Reckoner

(41) *al-Jalîl* = the Majestic

(42) *al-Karîm* = the Generous

(43) *al-Raqîb* = the Watcher

(44) *al-Mujîb* = the Approver

(45) *al-Wâsi'* = the All-Encompassing

(46) *al-Hakîm* = the Wise

(47) *al-Wadûd* = the Loving

(48) *al-Majîd* = the Glorious

(49) *al-Bâ'ith* = the Raiser

(50) *ash-Shahîd* = the Witness

(51) *al-Haqq* = the Truth

(52) *al-Wakîl* = the Advocate

(53) *al-Qawî'* = the Strong

(54) *al-Matîn* = the Firm

(55) *al-Walî* = the Patron

(56) *al-Hamîd* = the Praiseworthy

(57) *al-Muhsî* = the Counter

(58) *al-Mubdî* = the Beginner

(59) *al-Mu'îd* = the Restorer

(60) *al-Muhyî* = the Life-Giver

(61) *al-Mumît* = the Killer

(62) *al-Hayy* = the Living

(63) *al-Qayyûm* = the Subsisting

(64) *al-Wâjid* = the Finder

(65) *al-Mâjid* = the Magnificent

(66) *al-Wâhid* = the One and Only

(67) *as-Samad* = the Eternal

(68) *al-Qâdir* = the Powerful

(69) *al-Muqtadir* = the Prevailing

(70) *al-Muqaddim* = the Promoted

(71) *al-Mu'akhir* = the Deferrer

(72) *al-Awwal* = the First

(73) *al-Âkhir* = the Last

(74) *az-Zâhir* = the Outward

(75) *al-Bâtin* = the Inward

(76) *al-Wâlî* = the Governor

(77) *al-Muta'âlî* = the Exalted

(78) *al-Barr* = the Righteous

(79) *at-Tawwâb* = the Relenter

(80) *al-Muntaqim* = the Avenger

(81) *al-'Afûw* = the Pardoner

(82) *ar-Ra'ûf* = the Kind

(83) *Mâliku'l-Mulk* = the King of the Kingdom

(84) *dhu'l-Jalâli wa'l-Ikrâm* = full of Majesty and Bounty

(85) *al-Muqsit* = the Equitable

(86) *al-Jâmî'* = the Gatherer Together

(87) *al-Ghanî* = the Rich

(88) *al-Mughnî* = the Enricher

(89) *al-Mu'ti* = the Giver

(90) *al-Mâni'* = the Withholder

(91) *ad-Darr* = the Distresser

(92) *an-Nâfi'* = the Profiter

(93) *an-Nûr* = the Light

(94) *al-Hâdî* = the Guide

(95) *al-Badî'* = the Incomparable

(96) *al-Bâqî* = the Enduring

(97) *al-Warith* = the Inheritor

(98) *ar-Rashîd* = the Director

(99) *as-Sabûr* = the Patient

(9) Christian Sages

Fecisti nos ad te, et inquietum est cor nostrum donec requiescat in te.

Thou hast made us for Thyself, O Lord, and our hearts are restless till they rest in Thee.

Too late came I to love Thee, O uncreated Beauty, so ancient and so fresh, too late came I to love Thee. I sought Thee without, and behold Thou wast within me.

Ama et fac quod vis.

Love and do what thou wilt.

It is in the nature of the good to communicate itself.
Saint Augustine (354-430)

Lest it be thought that one as ignorant as I have fashioned these thoughts for myself, I do declare that they derive from my studies of the Arabs. I do not wish — should anything I say displease certain limited minds — to be the one who displeases them, for I know full well what the truly wise must expect from the common run of men. Therefore I take care not to speak for myself; I speak only for the Arabs.

Adelhard of Bath (Benedictine monk, beginning of 12th century)

The highest mineral virtue [gold] resides in man.

Saint Albert the Great [*Albertus Magnus*] (1193-1280)

Perfecta scientia Deum scire.

Perfect knowledge is to know God.

Saint Hilary (4th century)

Man is made for the contemplation of Heaven. Verily he is a heavenly plant, intended to come to the knowledge of God.

Clement of Alexandria [*Titus Flavius Clemens*] (c. 150-220)

The truth of the One God imposes itself by the superabundance of its clarity.

Truth is the ultimate goal of the whole universe and the contemplation of truth is the essential activity of wisdom. By their very nature, the virtues do not necessarily form part of contemplation, but they are an indispensable condition for it.

The principles of logic reside in God, and it is according to them that we must think.

The view is false which holds that it is indifferent, with regard to the truth of faith, whether one has a wrong opinion about creation, as long as one has a right opinion about God; for an error concerning creation engenders a false knowledge regarding God.

We must consider not only the emanation of a particular being from a particular agent, but also the emanation of all beings from the universal cause which is God: this emanation we designate by the name of creation. [*Summa Theologica*, I, 15, 1C]

. . . causing the distinction of things for the perfection of the whole, the same Divine Wisdom is also the cause of inequality. The universe would not be perfect were there but one level of goodness.

Dicendum quod sicut rationabilter procedere attribuitur naturali philosophiae, quia in ipse observatur maxime modus rationis, ita intellectualiter procedere attribuitur divinae sapientiae, eo quod in ipse observatur maxime modus intellectus.

41

It must be said that, just as proceeding *rationally* is attributed to natural philosophy, because in it there is clearly to be seen to the maximum degree the mode of reason, so proceeding *intellectually* is attributed to divine science because in it there is clearly to be seen to the maximum degree the mode of the Intellect. [*Boethium de Trinatate*, q. 6, art. 1-3]

What I have written seems to me to be like a wisp of straw compared with what I have seen and what has been revealed to me.

Saint Thomas Aquinas (1224-1274)

Bene scripsisti de Me Thoma.

Thou hast written well concerning Me, Thomas.

[*Words addressed by Christ to Saint Thomas Aquinas in a vision*]

---

reason (*ratio*):	— individual —	formal	— discursive
Intellect (*Intellectus*):	— universal —	supra-formal —	direct

---

Aliquid est in anima quod est increatum et increabile; si tota anima esset talis, esset increata et increabilis; et hoc est Intellectus.

There is something in the soul which is uncreated and uncreatable; if the whole soul were such, it would be uncreated and uncreatable; and this is the Intellect.

The Kingdom of God belongeth only to the thoroughly dead.

Sacramentum means a sign, and anyone who is content with merely a sign will never reach the inmost truth. But the seven sacraments all point to the One Reality. Marriage, for example, is a symbol of divine and human nature, an earnest of the union of the soul with God.

We can die gladly if God will live and work in us. . . . We die, it is true, but it is a gentle death.

Meister Eckhart (1260-1327)

By the light of the Intellect the human soul is illumined, as the world is illumined by the sun — nay, in yet fuller measure.

Hermes Trismegistos

One cannot be an accomplished philosopher unless one knows the philosophies of both Aristotle and Plato.

Saint Albert the Great [*Albertus Magnus*] (1193-1280)

Among the philosophers, Plato received the word of wisdom, and Aristotle received the word of science. The former considered principally the higher reasons, the latter, the lower reasons.

If there is anyone who is not enlightened by the sublime magnificence of created things, he is blind. If there is anyone who, seeing these works of God, does not praise Him, he is dumb. If there is anyone who, from so many signs, cannot perceive God, he is a fool.

Saint Bonaventure [*Giovanni de Fidanza*] (1221-1274)

Mens sine desiderio non intelligit;
mens sine intellectu non desiderat.

The mind without love cannot understand;
the mind without intelligence cannot love.

Nicholas of Cusa, Cardinal of Saint Pierre-aux-Liens (1401-1464)

Io veggio ben che giammai non si sazia
Nostro intelletto, se il ver non lo illustra.

I perceive that never can our Intellect be sated,
unless the Truth do shine upon it.

Paradiso, 4, 124-125

O voi, che avete gl'intelletti sani,
mirate la dottrina, che s'asconde
sotto il velame degli versi strani!

O ye, who have sane intellects,
see the doctrine that is hidden
beneath the veil of unfamiliar verses.

Inferno, 9, 61-63

A voce più ch'al ver drizzan li volti,
e così ferman sua opinione
prima ch'arte o ragion per lor s'ascolti.

They listen to assertions rather than to truth,
and in this way they form their opinions,
rather than letting art or reason be heard.

Purgatorio, 26, 121-123.

L'amor e 'l cuor gentil sono una cosa.

Love and the noble heart are the same thing.

Vita Nuova, Chap. 20

Tutti i miei pensier parlan d'amore!

All my thoughts speak of love!

Vita Nuova, Chap. 13

L'amor che muove il sole e le altre stelle.
The Love which moves the sun and the other stars.
Paradiso, 33, 145 (The last line of the *Divine Comedy*)

Dante (1265-1321)

(10) Christian Saints

Ama nesciri.

Love to be unknown (unrecognized, overlooked). [*His motto*]

Saint Bernard of Clairvaux (1090-1153)

Laudate et bendicete mi Signore, et rengratiate et serviate-li cun grande humilitate.

Praise and bless my Lord, and thank Him and serve Him with great humility.

Saint Francis of Assisi (1182-1226)

All other sins flee from God; pride alone sets itself up against Him.

Boethius (480-524)

All other sins attach themselves to evil, so that it may be done; only pride attaches itself to the good, so that it may be destroyed.

Saint Augustine (354-430)

Humility is to the virtues what the thread is to the rosary; take away the thread, and all the beads escape; take away humility, and all the virtues disappear.

The Curé d'Ars [Saint Jean-Baptiste Marie Vianney] (1786-1859)

Christ has no body now on earth but yours, no hands but yours, no feet but yours; yours are the eyes through which is to look out Christ's compassion on the world; yours are the feet with which he is to go about doing good; and yours are the hands with which he is to bless us now.

Those from whom I receive the greatest consolations and encouragement are those whom I know to be dwelling in Paradise.

Saint Theresa of Ávila (1515-1582)

Je choisis tout!
I choose all!

Je sentis la charité entrer dans mon coeur, le besoin de m'oublier pour faire plaisir et depuis lors je fus heureux!
I felt charity enter my heart, the need to forget myself in order to please others, and from that time on I was happy!

Dans le berceau de l'Église, ma Mère, je serai l'Amour.
In the cradle of the Church, my Mother, I will be Love.

Perfect love means putting up with other people's shortcomings, feeling no surprise at their weaknesses, finding encouragement even in the slightest evidence of good qualities in them.

Saint Theresa of Lisieux (1873-1897)

Elle était si belle que, lorsqu'on l'a vue une fois, on voudrait mourir pour La revoir!
She was so beautiful, that when one has seen her once, one would wish to die in order to see her again.

Saint Bernadette of Lourdes (1844-1879)

(11) Kings and Queens

Every king has a treasury; My treasury on earth is the heart of My believing slave.

Hadîth qudsî (Divine Saying)

How great is the power of prayer! It can be likened unto a queen, who has constant access to the king, and who can obtain from him anything she asks for.

Saint Theresa of Lisieux (1873-1897)

No one can understand a King but a king; therefore God has made each of us a king in miniature, so to speak, over a kingdom [namely our bodies, souls, and minds], which is an infinitely reduced copy of His own.

Al-Ghazâlî (1058-1111)

King of kings! And Lord of lords! And He shall reign for ever and ever!

**1 Timothy, 6, 15
(also Handel's Messiah)**

My Lord, eyes are at rest, the stars are setting, hushed are the movements of the birds in their nests, of the monsters in the deep. And Thou art the Just who knoweth no change, the Equity that swerveth not, the Everlasting that passeth not away. The doors of kings are locked and guarded by their henchmen. But Thy door is open to whoso calleth on Thee. My Lord, each lover is now alone with his beloved. And I am alone with Thee.

Hudhaifa al-'Adawîya (8th century)
(often attributed to Râbi'a al-'Adawîya)

(12) Miscellaneous Quotations

Magna est Veritas et praevalebit.

Great is the Truth and it shall prevail.

I Esdras, III, 18

Vincit omnia Veritas.

Truth conquers all.

I Esdras, 1, 12

Vincit omnia Amor.

Love conquers all.

Virgil (70-19 B.C.), Eclogue, iv, x, 69

Omne verum, a quocumque dicatur, Sancti Spiritus est.

Every truth, by whomsoever it is said, is of the Holy Spirit.

Saint Jerome (340-420)

Veritas temporis filia.

Truth is the daughter of time.

Aulus Gellius (c. 125-c. 181)

Truth will out.

English Proverb

Truth melteth like snow in the hands of him whose soul melteth not like snow in the hands of Truth.

attributed to Ahmad al-'Alawî (1869-1934)

They reckon ill who leave Me out.

Ralph Waldo Emerson (1803-1882) [in his poem *Brahma*]

The most serious disease that can attack a community is intellectual confusion and loss of overreaching purpose, which can only be provided by philosophy and religion.

The mind of the philosopher alone has wings, and this is just, for always, according to the measure of his abilities, he clings to the recollection of those things in which God abides. (*Phaedrus*)

A man who is good for anything ought not to calculate the chance of living or dying; he ought only to consider whether in doing anything he is doing right or wrong — acting the part of a good man or a bad one. (*Apology*)

Plato (427-347 B.C.)

Humanus sum; nihil humani a me alienum puto.

I am human; nothing that is human can I consider alien to me.

Terence (190-159 B.C.)

Nil admirari.

Be surprised at nothing.

Pythagoras (died 497 B.C.) [as reported by Plutarch]
given here in the Latin of Horace

Medio de fonte leporum
Surgit amari aliquid quod in ipsis floribus angat.

Amidst the fountain of delights there arises, from within the flowers themselves, something bitter that will choke them.

Lucretius (99-55 B.C.)

Nihil est ab omni parte beatum.

Nothing is perfect in every respect.

Horace (65-8 B.C.)

Rident stolidi verba latina.

Fools laugh at the Latin language.

Ovid (43-?17 B.C.)

If fools did not laugh at the *Tao*, it would not be the *Tao*.

Lao Tse (c. 570-490 B.C.)

A learned fool is worse than an ignorant fool.

We should look long and carefully at ourselves before we pass judgement on our fellows.

Molière (1622-1673)

Iudex damnatur ubi nocens absolvitur.

Take care that no one hates you justly.

The judge is condemned when the guilty is acquitted.

Bis dat qui cito dat.

He gives twice who gives quickly

Publilius Syrus (1st century B.C.)

A definition of orthodoxy:

Quod ubique, quod semper, quod ab omnibus creditum est.

That which has been believed everywhere, always, and by all.

Saint Vincent de Lérin (died c. 450 A.D.)

---

*The following three sayings remind us that there is such a thing as **objective truth** by which, in the end, man is judged.*

Every man acts according to his own way, but thy Lord knows best whose way is right.

Koran, Chapter "The Children of Israel", 17, 84

Quot homines, tot sententiae; suo quoque mos.

There are as many opinions as there are men; and for each man, this is his law.

Terence (190-159 B.C.)

Nothing is easier than self-deceit. For what each man wishes to believe, he believes to be true.

Demosthenes (384-322 B.C.), Third Olynthiac

When Pericles spoke, the people said: "How well he speaks."
When Demosthenes spoke, the people said: "Let us march!"

A definition of shamanism:
Sweet are the uses of adversity,
Which like the toad, ugly and venomous,
Wears yet a precious jewel in his head;
And this our life, exempt from public haunt,
Finds tongues in trees, books in the running brooks,
Sermons in stones, and good in everything.

The philosophy of Horatio:
There are more things in Heaven and earth, Horatio, than are
dreamt of in your philosophy.

William Shakespeare (1564-1616)

The mind can only repose on the stability of truth.

(*Of Voltaire and Rousseau*) Sir, it is difficult to settle the proportion
of iniquity between them.

The vast majority of men have no grounds for their opinions
except fashion; they follow the fashion of their day in all
matters.

Dr. Samuel Johnson (1709-1784)

Closer is He than breathing, nearer than hands and feet.

Alfred, Lord Tennyson (1808-1892)

We (God) are closer to man than his jugular vein.

Koran, Chapter "Qaf", 50, 16

As to the indulging of women in any particular liberties, it is
hurtful to the end of government and the prosperity of the city.

Aristotle (384-322 B.C.)

58

A definition of existentialism:
Hoc volo, sic jubeo, sic pro ratione voluntas.
I want it, I insist on it! Let my will stand instead of reason!

Maxima debetur puero reverentia
The greatest reverence is due to a child.
Juvenal (60-130)

Whoso shall offend one of those little ones . . . it were
better for him that a millstone be hanged about his neck,
and that he were drowned in the depth of the sea.
Matthew, 18, 6

Gutta cavat lapidem, non vi sed saepe cadendo.
The drop of water wears away the stone, not by violence but by
continually flowing. (*Tristia*, iv, x, 5, adapted by Hugh Latimer,
7th sermon before Edward VI, 1549)

Golden was that first age which, with no one to compel and
without a law, kept faith of its own will and did the right.
Ovid (43 B.C.-18 A.D.)

Perseverance is more prevailing than violence, and many
things which cannot be overcome when they are together, yield
themselves up when taken little by little.
Plutarch (c. 46-c. 120)

Beauty addresses itself chiefly to sight, but there is also a beauty
for hearing, as in certain combinations of words, and in all kinds
of music; for melodies and cadences are beautiful. Furthermore,
minds that lift themselves above the realm of the senses to a
higher order are aware of beauty in the conduct of life, in actions,

in character, in the pursuits of the intellect; and there is beauty in the virtues.

Plotinus (205-270)

Chi vuò, non può; chi può, non vuò,
Chi sa, non fa; chi fa, non sa,
E così il mondo mal va.

He who will, can not; he who can, will not; he who knows, does not; he who does, knows not. And thus does the world decline.

Italian Proverb

Si jeunesse savait, si vieillesse pouvait!
If only youth knew, if only age could!

French Proverb

The superior man expects everything from himself.
The inferior man expects everything from others.

Knowing others is intelligence; knowing yourself is true wisdom. Mastering others is strength; mastering yourself is true power.

If you realize that you have enough, you are truly rich. If you stay at the center and embrace death with your whole heart, you will live forever.

Lao Tse (c. 570-490 B.C.)

It is not good for men that they should obtain what they desire.

To fight passion is difficult, for what it requires has to be paid for at the price of the soul.

Heraclitus, fl. 5th century B.C. at Ephesus

Facilis descensus Averni; sed revocare gradum, hic labor est!

The descent to Avernus is easy; but to turn in one's tracks and go uphill, that is difficult!

Aeneid, vi, 126

Felix qui potuit rerum cognoscere causas.

Happy is he who can understand the causes of things.

Virgil (70-19 B.C.)
Georgics, ii. 490

A gem cannot be polished without friction, and a man cannot be perfected without trials.

Cicero (106-43 B.C.)

Gottesmühlen mahlen langsam, mahlen aber trefflich klein.

Friedrich von Logau (1605-1655),
Sinngedichte, III. ii. 24

The mills of God grind slowly, yet they grind exceeding small.

H. W. Longfellow (1807-1882),
Retribution

Es un entreverado loco, lleno de lúcidos intervalos.

He's a muddled fool, but he has lucid intervals.

Muchos pocos hacen un mucho.

Many a mickle mak's a muckle.

We cannot all be friars, but many are the ways by which God leads His children home.

Religion *is* knight-errantry (*or* chivalry [*caballería*]).

Del dicho al hecho hay gran trecho.
From speech to deed is a far cry indeed.
Miguel de Cervantes (1547-1616)

Without going out of my door, I can know all things on earth. Without looking out of my window, I can know the ways of Heaven.

The sage arrives without traveling, sees all without looking, does all without doing.
Lao Tse (c. 570-490 B.C.)

People of quality know everything without ever having been taught.
Molière (1622-1673)

We need not so much to be taught as to be reminded.
Dr. Samuel Johnson (1709-1784)

Books must be read as deliberately and reservedly as they were written.

Read the best books first, or you may not have the opportunity to read them at all.
Henry David Thoreau (1817-1862)

Reading — for a man devoid of prior understanding — is like a blind man looking in the mirror.
***Garuda Purâna*, 16, 82**

Verbum sapienti satis est.

One word is sufficient for the one who is wise.

Plautus (254-184 B.C.)

Mit der Dummheit kämpfen Götter selbst vergebens.

With stupidity even the gods struggle in vain.

Friedrich von Schiller (1759-1805)

Errare est humanum (**Saint Jerome**), *sed perseverare in errori per animositatem est diabolicum* (**Saint Augustine**).

To err is human (**Saint Jerome**), but to persist in error through malice is diabolical (**Saint Augustine**).

Le coeur a ses raisons que la raison ne connaît point.

The heart has its reasons which reason does not know.

Dieu est une sphère dont le centre est partout et la circonférence est nulle part.

God is a sphere whose center is everywhere and whose circumference is nowhere.

Blaise Pascal (1623-1662)

Misce stultitiam consiliis brevem;
Dulce est desipere in loco.

Mix in a little foolishness with your wisdom;
It is good to play the fool at the right time.

Horace (65-8 B.C.)

Poetry:
Monumentum aere perennius.

A monument more lasting than brass.

Horace (65-8 B.C.)

Tempora mutantur, nos et mutamur in illis.

Times change, and we too change with them.

Ovid (43 B.C.-18 A.D.)

Poetry is not a turning loose of emotion, but an escape from emotion; it is not the expression of personality, but an escape from personality.

Sentimentalism is caring for something more than God cares for it.

T. S. Eliot (1888-1964)

He who will not reason is a bigot; he who cannot is a fool; and he who dares not is a slave.

Sir William Drummond (1585-1649)

In town, manners were freer and pleasures more fervid, perhaps more perilous. . . . This is not saying that the literature of the last century (*i.e., the 18th century*) and before was not coarser than ours. It was — infinitely, and, to us, almost inconceivably coarse, but it had not the maleficent moral influence that is to be found in Ibsen and certain others. It spoke broadly of things as they were — openly of things natural, in a straightforward, farmyard kind of way; but it had no seductive sliminess, no artful suggestiveness about the sweetness of things sinful in themselves. It did not idealize the Abominable, and it did not warp the mind from reverence of the good by showing evil as a higher, because

64

a more "artistic" condition. Virtue was not then philistinism, and sin was not art; and crimes which are to the moral world what sewer-bred rats are to the material, were not dragged from their filthy hiding-places, and tricked out in tinsel and paste, as though they were divine things for men to worship and admire. Good principles were still considered necessary for the fit ordering of society, and when these fell slack, and evil consequences caused, there was lamentation and dismay, not idealization and a kind of fuliginous apotheosis.

Mrs. Eliza Lynn Linton (1822-1898)
(from "A Picture of the Past" in *The Nineteenth Century*, London, November 1892)

(13) Johann Wolfgang von Goethe (1749-1832)

Das Ewig-Weibliche zieht uns hinan.

The Eternal Feminine lifts us upward.

Faust, **closing line**

Allheit

Universality

Gottes ist der Orient!
Gottes ist der Okzident!
Nord- und südliches Gelände
ruht im Frieden seiner Hände.
Er, der einzige Gerechte,
will für jedermann das Rechte.
Sei von seinen hundert Namen
Dieser hochgelobet! Amen.

God's is the Orient!
God's is the Occident!
Northern and southern lands
rest in peace in His hands.
He who is the only Just,
wills justice for all.
Of all His hundred names,
Let this one be highly praised!
Amen.

Spanien

Spain

Herrlich ist der Orient
übers Mittelmeer gedrungen.
Nur wer Hafis liebt und kennt,
weiss was Calderon gesungen.

Most gloriously did the Orient
leap across the Mediterranean.
Only he who knows and loves Hâfiz,[1]
understands what Calderón[2] has sung.

Westöstlicher Diwan

The West-East Divan

[1] Mohammed Shams ad-Dîn (died 1389), better known as Hâfiz, was the greatest lyric poet of Persia.

[2] Pedro Calderón de la Barca (1600-1681), Spanish dramatist, author of *La Vida es Sueño.*

Lesebuch

Reading-book

Wunderlichstes Buch der Bücher　　Most wonderful book of books
Ist das Buch der Liebe.　　Is the Book of Love.
Aufmerksam hab ich's gelesen:　　I have read it carefully.
Wenig Blätter Freuden,　　It has few pages on happiness;
Ganze Hefte Leiden:　　But whole chapters on suffering.
Einen Abschnitt macht die　　Separation is given a section
Trennung,　　And reunion a short chapter.
Wiedersehn, ein klein Kapitel.　　It is fragmentary. There are
Fragmentarisch. Bände Kummern　　volumes on sorrows,
Mit Erklärungen erlängert,　　Made longer with explanations,
Endlos, ohne Maß.　　Endlessly, and beyond measure.
O Nisami! — doch am Ende　　O Nizami! — but in the end
Hast den rechten Weg gefunden:　　Thou hast found the right way:
Unauflösliches, wer löst es?　　The insoluble, who will solve it?
Liebende, sich wiederfindend.　　Those who love, and thereby find
　　themselves.

*

Mysticism is the heart of religion and the religion of the heart.
(*paraphrase*)

*

Denn alles, was entsteht, ist wert, dass es zugrunde geht.
All that becomes is destined to un-become.

*

There is no such thing as a liberal idea, only liberal sentiments.

*

A man should hear a little music, read a little poetry, and see
a fine picture every day of his life, so that worldly cares do not
obliterate the sense of the beautiful that God has implanted in
the human soul.

Goethe was a scientist as well as a poet; but when he was given an opportunity to look down a microscope, he refused to do so, because he did not wish to wrench from nature what she was unwilling to reveal to our natural senses. His mind-set was Platonic; he was only interested in understanding in depth. He had a clear intuition of the shallowness of modern scientific thought, and knew that, while it can show much ingenuity and complexity, in its substance it remains superficial.

(14) Democracy

Democracy passes into despotism.

Plato, *Republic,* **Part 4, Book 8.**

Let not the cobbler judge above his last.

Pliny [Gaius Plinius Secundus] (23-79)

Of all forms of government, democracy is the least accounted amongst civilized nations.

George Washington (1732-1799)
(1st President of the United States)

There was never a democracy yet that did not commit suicide.

John Adams (1735-1826)
(2nd President of the United States)

A democracy is never more than mob rule, where 51% of the people may take away the privileges of the other 49%.

Thomas Jefferson (1743-1826)
(3rd President of the United States)

Government by popular ignorance.

Elbert Green Hubbard (1856-1915)

The best argument against democracy is a five-minute conversation with the average voter.

Winston Spencer Churchill (1874-1965)

In actual fact, in present end-time conditions, there is no alternative to democracy. (At least in the Western industrialized countries.)

Communism and nazism have been "tried" — with disastrous results.

It is nevertheless essential to be aware of the ultimately fatal flaws of democracy, and not to let it become regarded as a panacea — or a god.

Such an awareness would of itself be a tremendous defense against these flaws.

(15) The Religion of the Sun Dance and the Sacred Pipe

We Indians know the one true God, and . . . we pray to Him continually.

Black Elk

We [Indians] never quarrel about religion, because it is a matter which concerns each man and the Great Spirit.

Red Jacket

We thank the Great Spirit for all the benefits that He has conferred upon us. I never take a drink of water from a spring, without being mindful of His goodness.

Black Hawk

The Sun Dance is the highest expression of our religion. All share in the fasting, in the prayer, and in the benefits. Some in the audience pray silently with the dancers. . . . The Sioux nation and all the peoples of the world are blessed by *Wakan Tanka*.

Fools Crow

Behold, my brothers, spring has come; the earth has received the embraces of the sun and we shall soon see the results of that love! Every seed is awakened and so has all animal life. It is through this mysterious power that we too have our being and we therefore yield to our neighbors, even our animal neighbors, the same right as ourselves, to inhabit this land.

Sitting Bull

When a man does a piece of work which is admired by all, we say that it is wonderful. But when we observe the succession of day and night, the sun, the moon, the stars in the sky, and the changing seasons on the earth, with their ripening fruits, one must see that it is the work of One who is more powerful than man.

Chased by Bears

Even the dress that you wore every day had a sacred meaning, and wherever you went or whatever you did, you were participating in a sacred life; you knew who you were and you carried a sense of the sacred with you. All of the forms had meaning, even the tipi and the sacred circle of the entire camp. . . . The support of the traditional life and the presence of Nature everywhere brought great blessings on all the people.

As we smoke the Pipe and offer our prayer with each new day, we should remember the importance of having a sacred center within us and that this sacred center is represented by the Pipe. It is the Sacred Pipe that connects us with God.

Yellowtail

(16) Hindu Quotations

Satyân nâsti paro dharmah.

There is no religion higher than the Truth.

Maxim of the Maharajas of Benares

There is no lustral water like unto Knowledge.

Bhagavad Gîtâ, IV, 38

Sages call the One Reality by many Names.

Rig Veda, I, 164, 46

Brahma satyam, jagan mithyâ; jîvo brahmaiva nâparah.

God is Reality, the world is appearance; the individual soul is not different from God.

from the Upanishads

Whoso, at the hour of death, leaves his body remembering Me, will be united with Me thereafter.

Bhagavad Gîtâ, VIII, 5

He who knoweth Him, knoweth himself, and is not afraid to die.

Atharva Veda, X, 8, 44

Creatures are made dear, not so that you may love creatures, but so that you may love God.

Brihadâranyaka Upanishad, II, 4, 5

Seated in a desert place, exempt from passion, master of his senses, let man represent to himself the Spirit, one and infinite, without allowing his thoughts to stray elsewhere.

Shankara (c. 788-820),
Âtmâ-Bodhi, **"Knowledge of the Spirit"**

Just as a fire appears to have a small or a great volume, and a beginning and an end — by being falsely identified with the burning wood — so *Âtmâ* appears to take on the attributes of the body by dwelling within it.

Shrimad Bhagavatam, **6, iv**

It is the *dharma* of water to flow, of fire to burn, of birds to fly, of fish to swim, and of man to achieve salvation.

Hindu saying

Riches and piety will diminish daily, until the world will be completely corrupted. In those days it will be wealth that confers distinction, passion will be the sole reason for union between the sexes, lies will be the only method for success in business, and women will be merely the objects of sensual gratification. The earth will be valued only for its mineral treasures, dishonesty will be the universal means of subsistence, a simple ablution will be regarded as sufficient purification. . . .

The observance of castes, laws, and institutions will no longer be in force in the Dark Age, and the ceremonies prescribed by the Vedas will be neglected. Women will obey only their whims and will be infatuated with pleasure. . . . Men of all kinds will presumptuously regard themselves as the equals of *brahmins*. . . . The *vaishyas* will abandon agriculture and commerce and will earn their living by servitude or by the exercise of mechanical professions. . . . The path of the Vedas having been abandoned, and man having been led astray from orthodoxy, iniquity will prevail and the length of human life will diminish in consequence.

... Then men will cease worshiping Vishnu, the Lord of sacrifice, Creator and Lord of all things, and they will say: "Of what authority are the Vedas? Who are the Gods and the *brahmins*? What use is purification with water?" The dominant caste will be that of *shûdras*. . . . Men, deprived of reason and subject to every infirmity of body and mind, will daily commit sins: everything which is impure, vicious, and calculated to afflict the human race will make its appearance in the Dark Age.

Vishnu Purâna **(3rd century A.D.)**

In the last days, perilous times shall come: men will love nothing but money and self; they will be arrogant, boastful, and abusive, with no respect for parents, no gratitude, no piety, no natural affection. . . . They will be men who put pleasure in the place of God, who preserve the outward form of religion, but are a standing denial of its reality. . . . Ever learning, but never able to come to a knowledge of the truth.

2 Timothy, **3, 1-7**

Lead me from the unreal to the Real;
Lead me from darkness to Light;
Lead me from death to Immortality.

Brihadâranyaka Upanishad, **I, 3, 27**

God and His name are one.

Ramakrishna (1836-1886)

(17) Buddhist Quotations

It is told that once Ânanda, the beloved disciple of the Buddha, saluted his master and said: "Half of the holy life, O master, is friendship with the beautiful, association with the beautiful, communion with the beautiful."

"Say not so, Ânanda, say not so!" the master replied. "It is not half the holy life, it is the whole of the holy life."

Samyutta Nikâyâ

The perfume of flowers goes not against the wind, not even the perfume of sandalwood, of rose-bay, or of jasmine; but the perfume of virtue travels against the wind and reaches unto the end of the world.

Dhammapada, 54

If a foolish man spends the whole of his life with a wise man, he never knows the path of wisdom as the spoon never knows the taste of soup. If a sensitive man spends a moment with a wise man, he soon knows the path of wisdom, as the tongue knows the taste of soup.

Dhammapada, 64-65

When the finger points at the moon, the foolish man looks at the finger.

Zen saying

A group of people were conversing about the future life. Some said that fish-eaters would be born into the Pure Land, others said that they would not. Hônen overheard them and said: "If it is a case of eating fish, cormorants would be born into the Pure Land, and if it is a case of not eating fish, monkeys would be so born. But I am sure that whether a man eats fish or not, if he only calls upon the Sacred Name, he will be born into the Pure Land."

It is useless to try to force to believe those who will not, for even the Buddha cannot do that.

Hônen (1133-1212)

(18) Christian Quotations

God does not ask for our blood, but for our faith.

We must please God by the posture of our body as well as by the measure of our voice.

Saint Cyprian of Carthage (d. 258)

The contemplation of Nature abates the fever of the soul, and banishes insincerity and presumption.

Saint Basil the Great (329-379)

When we hear that it is God who made everything, we must understand that God is in all things, and that He subsists as the essence of things.

Johannes Scotus Erigena (815-877)

Let the world indulge in its madness, for it cannot endure; it passes like a shadow. It is growing old and is, I believe, in its last decrepit stage. But we, buried deeply in the wounds of Christ, why should we be dismayed?

Saint Peter Canisius (1521-1597)

Non opus perfectum sed infinitum desiderium.

What matters is not so much a perfect work, but rather infinite love.

Saint Catherine of Siena (1347-1380)

All goodness is a loan from God.

Saint John of the Cross (1542-1591)

Mensch, werde wesentlich, denn wenn die Welt vergeht,
So fällt der Zufall ab; das Wesen, das besteht.

Man! Become "essentialized"! For when the world disappears,
Accidents fall away, and only Essence remains.

My heart could receive God if only it chose
to turn toward the Light as does the rose.

No thought for the hereafter have the wise,
for on this very earth, they live in Paradise.

The deepest prayer which I could ever say
is that which makes me one with That to which I pray.

If you could just be still, stop rushing round and round
in search of God — You'd find Him as your Ground.

The Name of Jesus is an oil poured out and spills,
It nourishes and shines, the soul's own woe it stills.

Angelus Silesius (1624-1677)

*

*   *

Deus noster refugium et virtus;	God is our refuge and our strength;
adjutor in tribulationibus	our help in the tribulations
quae invenerunt nos nimis.	that have overtaken us.

***Psalm*, 46, 1**

Ein' feste Burg ist unser Gott,	A mighty fortress is our God,
Ein gute Wehr und Waffen;	A trusty shield and weapon.
Er hilft uns frei aus aller Not,	He helps us free from every need
Die uns jetzt hat betroffen.	That has us now o'ertaken.

Martin Luther (1483-1546)

(19) Unity in Plurality, Plurality in Unity
Many Religions, One Truth

Other sheep I have that are not of this fold.

John, **10, 16**

In my Father's house are many mansions.
(*This applies not only in Heaven, but also on earth*: Sicut in Caelo **et in terra.**)

John, **14, 2**

And Peter opened his mouth and said: "Truly I perceive that God shows no partiality, and that anyone in any nation who fears Him, and does what is right, is acceptable to Him."

Acts, **10, 34-35**

[*After speaking with the Roman Centurion*] Verily I say unto you, I have not found such great faith, no, not in Israel. And I say unto you that many shall come from the east and the west, and shall sit down with Abraham and Isaac and Jacob in the kingdom of Heaven. But the children of the kingdom shall be cast out into outer darkness: there shall be wailing and gnashing of teeth.

Matthew, **8, 10-11**

A man's foes shall be they of his own household.

Matthew, **10, 36**

There is therefore one sole religion and one sole worship for all beings endowed with understanding, and this is presupposed through a variety of rites.

To different countries Thou hast sent different prophets and different masters, the ones at one time, the others at another time. But it is a law of our condition as men of this earth that a long habit becomes for us second nature, that it is taken for a truth and defended as such. It is from this that great dissensions arise, when each community opposes its own faith to other faiths.

And if it should be that it is impossible to remove this difference as to rites, and that this difference should even seem desirable in order to increase devotion (each religion attaching itself with more devotion to its ceremonies as if they had the more to please Thy Majesty), nevertheless, at least, as Thou art unique, there is but one religion and one worship.

Nicholas of Cusa, Cardinal of Saint Pierre-aux-Liens (1401-1464)
De Pace Fidei, 6, 1450

What folly to submit, because of religious sentimentalism, to demons, when it pertains to true religion to deliver us from the depravity that makes us like unto them!

Saint Augustine (354-430)
City of God, VIII, 17

When ye see a cloud rise out of the west, ye say, There cometh a shower; and so it is. And when ye see the south wind blow, ye say, There will be heat; and it cometh to pass. Ye hypocrites, ye can discern the face of the sky and of the earth, but how is it that ye do not discern this time?

Luke, 12, 54-56

That which today is called the Christian religion existed among the Ancients, and has never ceased to exist from the origin of the human race, until the time when Christ Himself came, and men began to call Christian the true religion which already existed beforehand.

Saint Augustine (354-430)
Epistles, **102: 11, 12 & 15**
De vera religione, **X, 19**

Never think or say that your religion is the best. Never denounce the religion of others. He who does so . . . with intent to enhance the glory of his own religion, in reality, by such conduct, inflicts the severest injury upon it.

King Ashoka (from his *Edicts*, India, 3rd century, B.C.)

(*On dispatching his Apostolic Delegate to Libya*)
Do not think that you are going amongst infidels. Muslims attain to salvation. The ways of God are infinite. (*L'Ultima*, Florence, VIII, 1934.)

Pope Pius XI [Achille Ratti] (1857-1939)

How consoling it is for me to know that, all over the world, there are millions of people who, five times a day, bow down before God.

The day is coming soon when the faithful will only be able to celebrate the holy sacrifice of the mass on the secret altar of the heart.

Pope Pius XII [Eugenio Pacelli] (1876-1958)

Appendices

APPENDIX I:
"It must needs be that scandals come."[1]

We live in an age that has seen the trajectories of such figures as Darwin, Marx, Freud, Jung, and Teilhard de Chardin. Some — or all — of these people may now be considered *passé*, but unquestionably their influence (perceived or unperceived) has left deep and lasting marks in our society. The main characteristics of this influence include progressivism, collectivism, psychologism, and scientism. Beyond any doubt these "-isms" are and remain the essential components of the received religion of today. What people refer to as the "religious bigotry" of past ages has been outdone — and by far — by the bigotry of the "religion" of the present age. Proof: one calls these modern beliefs into question at one's peril!

Very few persons and institutions have been left untouched by the trends and tendencies associated with the five names mentioned above. They are ubiquitous, and they show themselves, in different ways and to different degrees, in many and varied domains. Because of its importance in the Western world, it is relevant to consider how and to what extent these trends have affected the Roman Catholic Church. In fact, they have done so in the shape of the revolution that was the Vatican II council of 1962-1965. It is not too far-fetched to say that the behind-the-scenes architect of this council was the "ghost" of the already deceased Teilhard de Chardin.[2] The nature of the Vatican II revolution is most clearly revealed in the sayings and writings of the five post-Vatican-II popes themselves. Their program is

---

[1] "It must needs be that scandals come, but woe to that man by whom the scandal cometh" (*Matthew*, 18, 7).

[2] Teilhard de Chardin (1881-1955) was a French Jesuit. He was an ardent progressivist and promoted ideas which systematically contradicted the theses of scholastic philosophy as well as the Catholic catechism. His alleged findings in the field of paleontology were viewed with suspicion by his fellow paleontologists. He was forbidden to publish by Pope Pius XII, but on the death of the latter in 1958 his books were published and gained wide notoriety.

radical and unprecedented, but it has given rise to little concern on the part of an indifferent public.

A book of quotations of sages and saints is not the place for the utterances of the contemporary popes. But, since we live in an age in which black is white and white is black, drawing attention to this radical rejection of age-old wisdom, far from being out-of-place, may actually be beneficial. To this end, we have chosen to include, in the following Appendices, a few of the statements of two of the post-Vatican-II popes; it is best that they be allowed to speak for themselves.

APPENDIX II:
Giovanni Battista Montini (Pope Paul VI)

Extracts from *Paul VI* by Hubert Montheilhet
(Régine Deforges, Collection "*Nos Grands Hommes*", Paris, 1978)

The immensity of the break with tradition brought about by the Vatican II council (1962-1965) is not widely appreciated. The quotations below from Giovanni Battista Montini, the second of the five post-Vatican-II popes, indicate all too clearly just how radical the revolution was. His words are in direct opposition, not only to the traditional formulations of Saint Thomas Aquinas and other scholastic philosophers, but to Christianity in its very foundations.

At his audience on 2nd July 1969, Paul VI, with an exceptional clarity, declared: "One cannot avoid making the spontaneous reflection: 'If the whole world is changing, should not religion change also?'"

Opening the fourth session on 14th September 1965, he stated to the whole assembly: "The Council offers the Church . . . a panoramic vision of the world. Can the Church, and can we ourselves, do anything other than look upon the world and love it?"

But it is in his closing speech on 7th December 1965 that we find the core of the matter: "A current of love and admiration has overflowed from the Council onto the modern human world. . . . Its values have not only been respected, but honored; its efforts have been approved, its aspirations purified and blessed."

At his audience of 5th March 1969, Paul VI confided: "How does the Church look upon the world of today? The way the Church looks upon the world has been enlarged so as to modify appreciably the attitude that we have towards it. The doctrine of the Church has been enriched by a more complete knowledge of its nature and its mission. . . . This presupposes a different mentality, a mentality that we can describe as new."

Paul VI, with a particular eloquence, enthused at the most solemn moment of the Council, and I extract these passages from his closing speech on 7th December 1965: "All the doctrinal richness of the Council has but one aim: to serve man. . . . All things considered, does not the Council deliver a simple, new, and solemn lesson by teaching that we must love man in order to love God?. . . To know God, it is necessary to know man!. . . The discovery of human needs — and they are all the greater because the son of the earth has become greater! — has absorbed the attention of this synod. Recognize in it, you modern humanists who renounce the transcendence of supreme things, at least this merit, and know how to recognize our new humanism: We too, We more than anyone, We have the Cult of Man."

As Father Marcel de Corte has rightly said: "If the pope only flattered man from time to time, one could believe that it was merely a sporadic concession to the mania of the century. But he finds it necessary to do so at every turn. The observer cannot but note in him the presence of a *habitus*, as the scholastics would say, a fixed disposition, born of an original way of thinking, which, through continual use, has become ineradicable."

One cannot refrain from quoting here the words of the well-known hymn:

Change and decay in all around I see,
O Thou who changest not, abide with me!

APPENDIX III:
Joseph Ratzinger (Pope Benedict XVI)

The following quotations from Joseph Ratzinger, the fifth of the five post-Vatican-II popes, reveal only too clearly to what extent the time-honored teachings of Christianity have been wantonly brushed aside.

The impetus given by Teilhard de Chardin exerted a wide influence. With daring vision it incorporated the historical movement of Christianity into the great cosmic process of evolution.

Truth becomes a function of time. . . . Fidelity to yesterday's truth consists precisely in abandoning it in assuming it into today's truth.

The resurrection cannot be a historical event in the same sense as was the crucifixion.

from his book *Principles of Catholic Theology*

Following in the footsteps of my predecessors, in particular Paul VI and John Paul II, I feel intensely the need to affirm again the commitment assumed by Vatican II.

reported by *Zenit*, 25 April 2005

The point is that Christ's resurrection is something more, something different. If we may borrow the language of the theory of evolution, it is the greatest "mutation", absolutely the most crucial leap into a totally new dimension that there has ever been in the long history of life and its development: a leap into a completely new order which concerns us, and which concerns the whole of history.

from his Easter homily 2006

Eucharistic devotion such as is noted in the silent visit by the devout in church must not be thought of as a conversation with God. This would assume that God was present there locally and in a confined way. To justify such an assertion shows a lack of understanding of the Christological mysteries of the very concept of God. This is repugnant to the serious thinking of the man who knows about the omnipresence of God. To go to church on the ground that one can visit God who is present there is a senseless act which modern man rightly rejects.

from *Begründung Christlicher Existenz*

The Enlightenment is of Christian origin and it is no accident that it was born precisely and exclusively in the realm of the Christian faith. . . . It was the merit of the Enlightenment that it proposed anew these original values of Christianity, and gave back to reason its own voice. In the pastoral constitution "On the Church in the Modern World", the Vatican II Council once again underlined this profound correspondence between Christianity and the Enlightenment, seeking to come to a true conciliation between the Church and modernity. . . . It is necessary that both sides engage in self-reflection and be willing to correct themselves.

Lecture "Christianity: The Religion according to Reason" (Subiaco, Italy, 1 April 2005)

Ratzinger also says that Catholics are now free to reject the Syllabus of Errors of Pius IX, because "Vatican II is a counter-syllabus".

Father Joseph Sainte-Marie in *Catholic Family News*, **July 2000**

If anyone says that the dogmas evolve, let him be anathema.

Pope Pius X [Giuseppe Melchiorre Sarto] (1835-1914)

Note

The most informative book about the Vatican II Council is *The Destruction of the Christian Tradition* by Dr. R. P. Coomaraswamy (World Wisdom Books, Bloomington, Indiana, second edition, 2006), from which the quotations by Cardinal Ratzinger were taken.

APPENDIX IV:
A Message of Hope

The three preceding Appendices — on the Vatican II Council and the post-Vatican II popes — make depressing reading. It therefore seems necessary to recall that Christ prophesied that his Church (Christianity in its various traditional forms, Eastern and Western) would exist to the end of time. Roman Catholicism, for its part, continues unchanged in the form of the traditionalist clergy and faithful who, as small groups in many different countries, reject Vatican II and retain authentic doctrines and valid sacraments. Together with the venerable Churches of the Christian East (and not forgetting original and pre-liberal Protestantism), "the gates of hell will not prevail against it".

As is well-known, the non-Christian religions too have suffered both from secularism on the one hand, and from false "fundamentalism" on the other. But, despite everything, the present anthology of quotations, drawn from the "invincible wisdom" of all authentic religions and philosophies is, against the spirit of the times, a powerful message of hope and a profound inward consolation.

ENVOI

"Think on these things"

Envoi to the reader of these quotations

Whatsoever things are true, whatsoever things are honest, whatsoever things are just, whatsoever things are pure, whatsoever things are lovely, whatsoever things are of good report; if there be any virtue, and if there be any praise, *think on these things.*

Philippians, **4, 8**

INDEX

www.ingramcontent.com/pod-product-compliance
Lightning Source LLC
LaVergne TN
LVHW091154080426
835509LV00006B/677